Public Library District of Columbia

12 REASONS TO LOVE THE
WASHINGTON NATIONALS

by Bo Smolka

12 STORY LIBRARY

www.12StoryLibrary.com

12-Story Library is an imprint of Peterson Publishing Company and Press Room Editions.

Produced for 12-Story Library by Red Line Editorial

Photographs ©: John Hefti/Icon Sportswire/AP Images, cover, 1, 19; Jacquelyn Martin/AP Images, 4; Pablo Martinez Monsivais/AP Images, 5, 11, 16, 28, 29; Bill Grimshaw/AP Images, 6; Otto Greule Jr./Getty Images, 8; Gregory Smith/AP Images, 10; Bettmann/Corbis, 13; Mark Goldman/Icon SMI/Corbis, 14; Richard Lipski/AP Images, 18; Alex Brandon/AP Images, 20, 24; Marcio Jose Sanchez/AP Images, 23; Alex Brandon/AP/Corbis, 27

ISBN
978-1-63235-218-7 (hardcover)
978-1-63235-245-3 (paperback)
978-1-62143-270-8 (hosted ebook)

Library of Congress Control Number: 2015934324

Printed in the United States of America
Mankato, MN
October, 2015

12 STORY LIBRARY

Go beyond the book. Get free, up-to-date content on this topic at 12StoryLibrary.com.

TABLE OF CONTENTS

NATIONALS ARE WALK-OFF WINNERS

The Washington Nationals opened their new ballpark with a bang. When they moved to Washington in 2005, the Nationals played at RFK Stadium. It was a drab, old building that had seen better days. In recent years it had been used mainly for football and soccer.

In 2008, the Nationals moved into Nationals Park. They finally had a ballpark to call their own. A sellout crowd poured in to see the Nationals face the Atlanta Braves on March 30, 2008. It was the season opener. From the top of the upper deck, fans could see the Capitol dome. That left no doubt that this was Washington's stadium. President George W. Bush was at the game. He threw out the ceremonial first pitch.

The crowd had plenty to cheer about right away. The Nationals took a 2–0 lead in the first inning. They led 2–1 going into the ninth inning. But then Atlanta tied the game.

Nationals Park before the Nationals' 2008 home opener

With the score 2–2 in the bottom of the ninth, Nationals third baseman Ryan Zimmerman stepped up to bat. Zimmerman was already a fan favorite. He had hit a team-high 24 home runs the year before. His picture was on a big billboard outside Nationals Park. He was the face of the franchise.

Zimmerman lined a pitch to left-center field. The Braves' center fielder raced back. He looked up. Home run! The Nationals won 3–2. Zimmerman circled the bases as the crowd roared. Nationals owner Mark Lerner called the walk-off home run a "storybook ending."

Ryan Zimmerman celebrates his walk-off home run in the 2008 home opener.

THINK ABOUT IT

How much do you think fan support affects baseball players? Do you believe Ryan Zimmerman would have hit that home run had the Nationals been playing in their old stadium? What if they were playing on the road?

39,389
Attendance at Nationals Park for the 2008 season opener.

- Pitcher Odalis Perez started the game for Washington.
- Closer Jon Rauch recorded the win, even though he gave up the tying run in the ninth.

MONTREAL JOINS THE MAJOR LEAGUES

The Washington Nationals did not begin in Washington. The team did not even begin in the United States. In 1969, the Nationals began as an expansion team in Montreal, Canada. They were known as the Montreal Expos. It was the first Major League Baseball (MLB) team located outside the United States.

The Expos went their first 10 years without a winning season. But by the late 1970s, things began looking up.

In 1977, Expos outfielder Andre Dawson had a memorable debut. He hit .282 with 19 home runs. He was named the National League (NL) Rookie of the Year. Dawson and 23-year-old catcher Gary Carter were cornerstones for a team on the rise.

In 1979, Montreal went 95–65.

Montreal Expos catcher Gary Carter salutes the crowd after a playoff win in 1981.

It was the team's first winning season.

In 1981, the Expos enjoyed another first: a trip to the postseason. That season had been interrupted by a labor strike. For two months, no major league games were played. The strike ended in August. Because of the long break, the season was split into two halves.

The Expos won the NL East second half with a record of 30–23. They faced the NL East's first-half champion, the Philadelphia Phillies, in a Divisional Series. The Expos won the best-of-five series, three games to two. They advanced to the NL Championship Series (NLCS),

52

Games won by the 1969 Montreal Expos. It remains the worst season in team history.

- The Expos won at least 90 games in four different seasons but didn't make the playoffs in any of them.
- Gary Carter and Andre Dawson were both inducted into the Baseball Hall of Fame.

where they lost to the Los Angeles Dodgers. But playoff baseball had come to Montreal.

JACKIE ROBINSON IN MONTREAL

Baseball was in Montreal long before the Expos. In 1946, Jackie Robinson played for the Montreal Royals. They were the top minor league team of the Brooklyn Dodgers. Robinson, who was black, became the Royals' star player. He led the team to the International League title. The next spring, Robinson broke MLB's color barrier and joined the Dodgers. "The people of Montreal were warm and wonderful to us," Robinson recalled years later.

THE EXPOS STRIKE OUT IN 1994

After the 1981 season, the Expos did not win another divisional title. However, they were on their way to one in 1994. That July, the Expos had an eight-game winning streak. They took the lead in the NL East.

By early August, their lead had grown to seven games.

Ken Hill and a future star named Pedro Martinez were a dynamic duo on the mound. Outfielder Moises Alou hit .339 with 22 home runs. It seemed as if nothing could stop them.

As the season rolled on, though, baseball team owners and players began bickering about how much players should be paid. To protest, the players

The Expos' Moises Alou bats in a 1994 game.

went on strike. They refused to play. After August 11, there were no more games that season. The Expos' great season had come to a screeching halt.

The Expos finished with a record of 74–40. The .649 winning percentage was the team's best ever in Montreal. But there were no playoffs. For the first time since 1904, there was no World Series. The Expos could only wonder what might have been.

The 1994 season was the beginning of the end of baseball in Montreal. Some top players were traded after the season. The team finished last in the NL East the next year. Its budget dwindled. Attendance dropped. Top free agents did not want to play in Montreal.

By 2004, the team had been sold. It was nearly shut down. By then, the team was being run by MLB. The Expos even played some home games in Puerto Rico. If the team had any future, it would not be in Montreal.

22
Home games the Expos played in Puerto Rico in 2003 and 2004.

- From 1992 on, Montreal's Olympic Stadium could seat 46,500 fans for baseball games.
- The average attendance at Olympic Stadium in 2004 was just 9,009.

ALL IN THE FAMILY

Felipe Alou was the manager of the 1994 Expos. His son Moises Alou was the team's star outfielder. And the Alou family ties in baseball were even stronger. Felipe and his brothers Matty and Jesus Alou all played in the major leagues. On September 15, 1963, with the San Francisco Giants, they became the only set of brothers to play outfield together in the major leagues. They played together two more times that month.

BASEBALL RETURNS TO WASHINGTON

Washington DC is the US capital. Baseball is known as the United States' national pastime. But for more than 30 years, there had been no MLB team in Washington. That finally changed in 2005. MLB announced in the fall of 2004 that the Montreal Expos would move to Washington.

"It's a great day for Washington," mayor Anthony Williams declared. Fans met at a Washington pep rally and sang "Take Me Out to the Ball Game."

To baseball-starved fans in Washington, it did not matter that they were getting a team that had lost 95 games the year before. It did not matter that the team had to

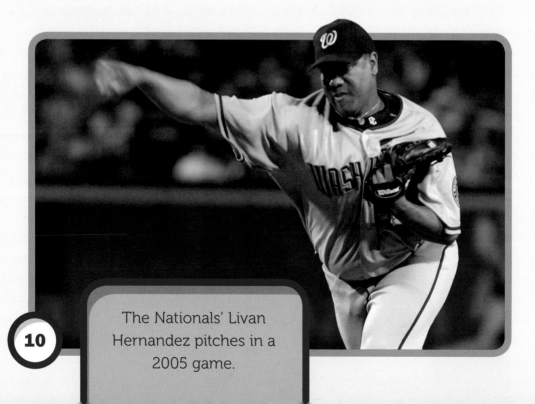

The Nationals' Livan Hernandez pitches in a 2005 game.

Fans cheer before the Nationals' first game in 2005.

play in dingy RFK Stadium for the first few seasons. It did not matter that the team lacked star players. All that mattered was that the MLB was back in Washington.

With the new home came new uniforms, a new logo, and a new name: the Nationals.

Frank Robinson, who had managed the team in Montreal, remained as manager. And the Nationals gave fans a lot to cheer for right away. The team had a five-game winning streak in April. It had a 10-game winning streak in June. And at the All-Star Break, the Nationals led the NL East. The Nationals faded down the stretch. But their final record of

81–81 was much better than many people had expected. Baseball indeed was back in Washington.

63

Days the Nationals spent in first place in 2005.

- Outfielder Jose Guillen was the Nationals' top hitter.
- He batted .283 with 24 home runs and 76 runs batted in (RBIs).
- Livan Hernandez was the top pitcher with a 15–10 record.

THE NATIONAL PASTIME THRIVES IN THE NATION'S CAPITAL

There had been major league baseball in Washington DC long before the Nationals. There just wasn't much good baseball.

The Washington Senators lost 113 games in 1904. They lost 110 in 1909. Seasons like that led writer Charles Dryden to proclaim that Washington was "first in war, first in peace, and last in the American League."

It wasn't always awful. Hall of fame pitcher Walter Johnson led the Senators to the World Series title in 1924. They again reached the World Series in 1925. But

NEGRO LEAGUES SUCCESS

Some of the best players in Washington at that time were not in the major leagues. They instead played in the Negro Leagues. Up until the late 1940s, blacks were not welcome in the major leagues. So Negro Leagues formed in cities with large black populations. That included Washington. The Homestead Grays were one of the top Negro Leagues teams. They played in Washington in the 1940s. They shared the Senators' Griffith Stadium. The Grays often drew bigger crowds than the Senators. Grays catcher Josh Gibson blasted some of the longest home runs ever hit at Griffith Stadium. He was known as "the black Babe Ruth."

1
World Series titles the Washington Senators won.

- They appeared in three World Series.
- They also had 10 100-loss seasons.
- The Senators finished last in the league 13 times.

90-loss seasons were far more common. The Senators moved to Minnesota after the 1960 season. That team became the Minnesota Twins. Washington got an expansion team the next year. But it did not fare much better. In 11 seasons, that team had just one winning season. Hall of famer Ted Williams was the Senators' manager from 1969 to 1971. After a 96-loss season in 1971, the Senators moved to Texas. They became the Texas Rangers. That was the last Washington saw of major league baseball until the Nationals came to town.

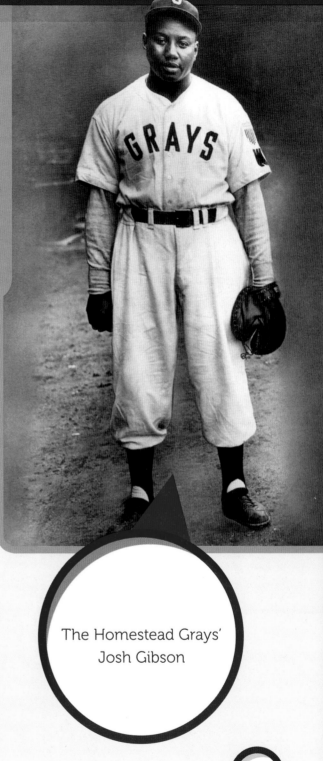

The Homestead Grays' Josh Gibson

ON YOUR MARK, GET SET . . . THE RACING PRESIDENTS

6

George Washington, Abraham Lincoln, Thomas Jefferson, and Theodore Roosevelt were all US presidents long ago. They never saw a Nationals game. But they are all a big part of Nationals tradition.

During the fourth inning of each Nationals home game, mascots representing US presidents race from center field toward the Nationals dugout. Each mascot wears a giant foam head that looks like one of six former presidents: Washington, Lincoln, Roosevelt, Jefferson, William Howard Taft, and Calvin Coolidge. They each have their own Nationals jersey.

The race has become one of the highlights of every game. Fans go wild as the cartoonish-looking presidents waddle toward the finish line. A race announcer describes every step.

The Racing Presidents have become popular all over town. They have

The Racing Presidents in 2014

PRESIDENTS AND BASEBALL

US presidents have a long history with baseball in Washington. President William Howard Taft was the first president to throw out a ceremonial first pitch. He did that in 1910. Taft also may have started the seventh-inning stretch. Legend has it that Taft, who was very heavy, grew uncomfortable sitting in a rickety seat at a Washington Senators game. So in the seventh inning, he stood up to stretch. Since the president stood up, everyone else stood up as well.

shown up at big parades. They have even been invited to the White House.

For several years, Roosevelt, known as "Teddy," never won. Sometimes he would be tripped near the finish line. Or he would be distracted just before winning. He became the team's lovable loser. Teddy's losing streak made national news. Would Teddy ever win? Then on October 3, 2012, the other presidents were all knocked over during the race. Teddy won!

That was the last day of the 2012 season. It was a season of firsts for the Nationals. They made the

playoffs for the first time. And Teddy finally won a race.

1

Jersey number worn by the George Washington mascot, since he was the first US president.

- The other presidents have jersey numbers that match the order of their presidency.
- Thomas Jefferson is No. 3, Abraham Lincoln is No. 16, Theodore Roosevelt is No. 26, William Howard Taft is No. 27, and Calvin Coolidge is No. 30.

15

NATIONALS FANS SAY MERRY "STRASMAS"

The Nationals trudged through the 2008 season with a record of 59–102. It was the worst record in the majors. But that gave them the first pick in the 2009 draft. With that pick, they selected a flame-throwing pitcher from San Diego State University named Stephen Strasburg. He once had struck out 23 players in a college game.

Even in the minor leagues, hype followed Strasburg everywhere. His starts drew huge crowds.

Almost exactly one year after he was drafted, Strasburg joined the Nationals.

A crowd of more than 40,000 filled Nationals Park for Strasburg's debut. Eager fans referred to his arrival as "Strasmas." Flash bulbs from cameras popped as Strasburg fired his first pitch. He struck out 14 players that day, including the last seven batters he faced. The Nationals won 5–2.

Stephen Strasburg pitches in his MLB debut in 2010.

THINK ABOUT IT

Should Stephen Strasburg have pitched in the 2012 playoffs? If you were general manager, what would you have done?

95.5

Average miles per hour (154 km/h) of Stephen Strasburg's fastball.

- Strasburg played for Team USA at the 2008 Olympics in China.
- He helped Team USA win a bronze medal.

Strasburg went 5–3 that season. But then he injured his arm. He needed to have surgery. He missed almost all of the 2011 season.

In 2012, Strasburg seemed better than ever. He went 15–6. But his season again ended early. The Nationals front office did not want Strasburg throwing too much so soon after surgery. The team decided in the spring to limit Strasburg to about 160 innings. So even with the team in first place, he was shut down at 159.1 innings.

The Nationals lost in the playoffs. Would they have won with Strasburg pitching? No one will ever know. But the question haunts Nationals fans.

Strasburg has struggled with injuries and inconsistency since that season. But he has shown flashes of brilliance. His 3.00 earned-run average (ERA) in 2013 was the best of any full season he pitched. And in 2014, he led the league with 242 strikeouts and 32 starts.

STICKING TO THE PLAN

The Nationals stood by their decision to shut down Stephen Strasburg late in the 2012 season. "We had a plan in mind," general manager Mike Rizzo said. "It was something we had from the beginning. I stand by my decision. We'll take the criticism as it comes. We have to do what's best for the Washington Nationals, and we think we did."

BRYCE HARPER IS "BASEBALL'S CHOSEN ONE"

The Nationals had the worst record in the MLB for the second straight year in 2009. So they again had the first pick in the draft in 2010. They selected a brash 17-year-old named Bryce Harper.

By then, Harper had already become something of a legend. When he was three, he played T-ball with boys three years older. In 2005, *Baseball America* named him "possibly the country's best 12-year-old hitter." He destroyed high school pitching. He went to all-star games and hit towering home runs. And in 2009, at age 16, Harper was on the cover of *Sports Illustrated.* The magazine labeled him "Baseball's Chosen One."

Harper graduated from high school early and went to junior college. He thought that would help him reach the major leagues more quickly.

Bryce Harper slides into third base during a 2012 game.

22

Home runs Bryce Harper hit as a rookie with the Nationals in 2012.

- He batted .270 and added 59 RBIs.
- Harper was named the NL Rookie of the Year.

Some people did not like Harper's style. He slathered on eye black to look like a warrior. To some, he came across as cocky. But he was unstoppable. Harper played one season at the College of Southern Nevada, and he dominated.

Harper was a 6-foot-3 catcher with speed, power, and a cannon for an arm. Scouts drooled over him. But the Nationals decided Harper would not be a catcher. After he was drafted, they moved him to the outfield. They thought that would help prevent injuries that could shorten his career.

Early signs looked good. Harper debuted with the Nationals in 2012. He quickly established himself as a key player on a team that made the playoffs in 2012 and 2014. And he showed signs of maturing in his first few seasons. By 2015, Harper was a bona fide star. He opened the season by hitting six home runs over three games in May, and he had 13 total home runs for the month. At just 22 years old, his potential seemed limitless.

Bryce Harper prepares to swing during the 2014 playoffs.

19

"NATITUDE" WINS THE DIVISION

When the 2012 season began, the Nationals were generating buzz in Washington. Those 100-loss seasons were behind them. They had gone 80–81 the year before. Young pitcher Stephen Strasburg once again was healthy. And outfielder Bryce Harper, who was just 19 years old, was on his way to the major leagues. He joined the team in late April. Around town, billboards and ads touted the team's "Natitude."

But the Nationals had more than that dynamic duo. They also had a veteran manager in Davey Johnson. They had a good young pitching staff. And the infield featured popular third baseman Ryan Zimmerman and first baseman Adam LaRoche. Both could hit the ball a long way.

Most observers thought the Nationals were still a year away from contending for the championship. But the players didn't believe that. At

Nationals players greet Jayson Werth after his walk-off home run in the 2012 playoffs.

the All-Star break, they had a record of 49–34. They led the NL East by four games. People kept waiting for the Nationals to fade. Instead, they reeled off eight straight wins and won the division with a 98–64 record.

The Nationals' first playoff appearance ended in heartbreaking fashion, though. They faced the St. Louis Cardinals in the first round. The five-game series came down to the final game. The Nationals took a 6–0 lead. They still led 7–5 going into the ninth inning. But then the Nationals' usually rock-solid bullpen faltered. The Cardinals scored four runs to win 9–7.

21

Wins by Nationals pitcher Gio Gonzalez in 2012, which led all of MLB and set a team record.

- All five Nationals starting pitchers won at least 10 games.
- First baseman Adam LaRoche led the team with 33 home runs and 100 RBIs.

But the Nationals served notice. They were no longer pushovers. They were here to stay.

WERTH THE WAIT

The Nationals trailed the St. Louis Cardinals two games to one in their best-of-five playoff series. They needed to win Game 4 or their season would be over. With the game tied 1–1 in the ninth inning, Jayson Werth stepped up to the plate. He fouled off pitch after pitch from Cardinals reliever Lance Lynn. Then on the 13th pitch of the at-bat, Werth drilled a belt-high pitch over the left-field fence. Home run! The Nationals survived. It remains one of the most memorable moments in Nationals history.

WASHINGTON IS BACK ON TOP IN 2014

Two years after winning their first division title, the Nationals won another in 2014. In late July, they were locked in a battle with the Atlanta Braves. The Nationals led by a half-game on July 30. Then they went 39–19 the rest of the way. With a 96–66 record, they ran away with the division. Washington won by a whopping 17 games.

Third baseman Anthony Rendon emerged as a star. He hit .287 with 21 home runs. His 111 runs scored led the NL. Center fielder Denard Span hit .302 and set a Nationals record with 184 hits. First baseman Adam LaRoche drove in 92 runs.

But the biggest reason for the Nationals' success was on the mound. Washington had a team ERA of 3.03. That was the best in the majors.

Doug Fister had a team-best 16 wins. Three starters had ERAs under 3.00. And Stephen Strasburg led the NL with 242 strikeouts.

In the playoffs, though, the Nationals suffered more heartbreak. They lost the first two games at home to the San Francisco Giants. In Game 2,

10

Length of the Nationals' winning streak in August 2014, which tied the team record.

- The team had five walk-off wins during the streak, three of them in a row.
- They won seven of the 10 games by just one run.
- Despite the winning streak, the Nationals' lead in the division improved by only three games.

35,085 at Nationals Park was on its feet. Fans were cheering every pitch. The first Marlins batter in the ninth inning grounded out. The next flied out. Still, there were no hits. Up stepped Christian Yelich. He was one of the Marlins' best hitters. Yelich drove a pitch toward the gap in left-center field.

Zimmermann could not believe it. As the ball sailed toward the fence, Zimmermann just looked to the sky. *Double*, he thought. *No doubt. Double.*

Steven Souza saw the ball, too. Souza had just entered the game as the Nationals' left fielder. He had begun the season in the minor leagues. He had only played about 20 games all season with the Nationals. Souza raced back as fast as he could. Just before the warning track, Souza leaped. He went flying through the air and reached up with his glove. He caught the ball!

Zimmermann had done it. He had pitched the first no-hitter in Nationals history. And Souza had made the catch of a lifetime.

104

Pitches thrown by Jordan Zimmermann in his 2014 no-hitter.

- He struck out 10 batters while walking one.
- Zimmermann finished the year with a 14–5 record.

MORE NO-NOS

Jordan Zimmermann threw the first no-hitter in Washington Nationals history. It wasn't the first in franchise history, though. Montreal Expos pitchers tossed four no-hitters. Bill Stoneman was the first to do so. In fact, he did it twice. Stoneman no-hit the Philadelphia Phillies in 1969 and the New York Mets in 1972. Charlie Lea no-hit the San Francisco Giants in 1981. Ten years later in 1991 Dennis Martinez threw a perfect game against the Los Angeles Dodgers. That meant he retired all 27 batters in order. No one reached base on a hit, walk, or error. It was only the 13th perfect game in MLB history.

THERE IS NO STOPPING SCHERZER

The Nationals tasted success with a division title in 2014. The pieces appeared to be in place for a run to the World Series in 2015. Then the team went out and signed one of the best pitchers in baseball.

Max Scherzer was a true ace. He was a 2013 Cy Young Award winner with the Detroit Tigers. His powerful fastball could cut just before reaching the plate. Batters—especially right-handers—had little hope for getting a hit.

Scherzer lived up to his billing. Midway through the 2015 season, he completed one of the most dominant three-game stretches in history. Scherzer threw 26 innings while giving up just two runs. He struck out 33 batters, walked one, and allowed just six hits. Scherzer was one pitch away from a perfect game in the second of those three games. However, he hit a batter and instead settled for a no-hitter.

The season proved to be a disappointment for the Nationals, however. Key players struggled. The New York Mets ran away with the division title. But in the second-to-last game, Scherzer delivered again. Facing the Mets, Scherzer began mowing down hitters. He threw 109 pitches over nine innings. Scherzer faced 28 batters. Seventeen struck

9

Batters who struck out of the final 10 outs in Max Scherzer's no-hitter against the Mets.

- That was just one shy of the MLB record of 10 strikeouts in a row.
- Scherzer's 276 strikeouts in 2015 ranked second in the majors.

A teammate covers Max Scherzer in chocolate sauce in celebration of Scherzer's no-hitter against the Pittsburgh Pirates in June 2015.

out. No one walked. No one got a hit, either. The only player to reach base did so on an error.

The game was Scherzer's second no-hitter of the season. He became only the fifth pitcher to throw two no-hitters in one regular season. Some experts called it the most impressive no-hitter ever.

THINK ABOUT IT

Why do you think Max Scherzer's no-hitter against the Mets was so impressive? What did he do that set himself apart from other no-hitters? Are there any instances in which a no-hitter is not very impressive?

12 KEY DATES

1901

The Washington Senators begin play in the same year the American League (AL) begins. In the midst of many losing seasons, the Senators reach three World Series. But the team moves to Minnesota in 1961 and becomes the Twins.

1961

A new Washington Senators team begins play in the AL, but after 11 seasons, it moves to Texas in 1972 to become the Rangers.

1969

The Montreal Expos begin play as the first MLB team located outside the United States.

1981

The Expos make the NL playoffs for the first and only time. However, they lose to the Los Angeles Dodgers in the NLCS.

1994

Just after the midway point of the season, the Expos lead the NL East with a 74–40 record. But a players' strike ends the season and the World Series is canceled. Fans can only wonder how the best season in Expos history might have ended.

2003

The Expos begin a two-year stretch in which they play 22 home games in Puerto Rico.

2005

The Expos move to Washington and become the Nationals. They play their first three seasons at RFK Stadium.

2008

Nationals Park opens as the team's new ballpark. In the season opener, President George W. Bush throws out the ceremonial first pitch, and the Nationals beat the Atlanta Braves 3–2 on a walk-off home run by third baseman Ryan Zimmerman.

2010

Former first overall draft pick Stephen Strasburg strikes out 14 Pittsburgh Pirates and leads the Nationals to a 5–2 win on June 8 in his first major league start.

2012

Former first overall draft pick Bryce Harper wins the NL Rookie of the Year Award after hitting 22 home runs and driving in 59 runs for the Nationals.

2012

The Nationals reach the NL playoffs for the first time since moving to Washington but lose to the St. Louis Cardinals in the first round.

2015

Over three games, the Nationals' Max Scherzer pitches 26 innings, giving up just six hits and two earned runs while striking out 33 batters and walking just one. The second game in that stretch was a no-hitter against the Pittsburgh Pirates.

GLOSSARY

ace
The best pitcher on a baseball team.

draft
A system leagues use to spread incoming talent among all the teams. The teams pick players in order of how they finished the previous season, with the worst team picking first.

earned-run average
The number of earned runs a pitcher or team gives up over nine innings.

expansion team
A brand new team.

hype
Excitement.

labor strike
When people refuse to work because they object to working conditions.

mascot
A person or character who represents a team.

no-hitter
A game in which a pitcher or a team allows no hits. If the pitcher or team allows no base runners, including on errors, it's a perfect game.

protest
An action or statement meant to express disapproval.

rookie
A first-year player.

scout
A person who studies players and advises a team's front office about them.

warning track
A wide strip of dirt that runs near the outfield fence. Since outfielders are often looking up to track a ball, the warning track helps them know when they are close to the wall.

FOR MORE INFORMATION

Books

Miech, Rob. *Phenom: The Making of Bryce Harper.* New York: St. Martin's Press, 2012.

Povich, Shirley. *The Washington Senators.* Kent, OH: Kent State Press, 2010.

Smith, Elliot. *Beltway Boys: Stephen Strasburg, Bryce Harper and the Rise of the Washington Nationals.* Chicago: Triumph Books, 2013.

Websites

Baseball Reference
www.baseball-reference.com

National Baseball Hall of Fame
www.baseballhall.org

Washington Nationals
www.washington.nationals.mlb.com

INDEX

About the Author

Bo Smolka is a former sports copyeditor at the *Baltimore Sun* and former sports information director at Bucknell University, his alma mater. He grew up in Washington DC and now lives in Baltimore with his wife and two children.

READ MORE FROM 12-STORY LIBRARY

Every 12-Story Library book is available in many formats, including Amazon Kindle and Apple iBooks. For more information, visit your device's store or 12StoryLibrary.com.